W9-BIQ-914

Date: 01/25/12

SP J 508.2 SCH
Schuette, Sarah L.,
Veamos la primavera = Let's
look at spring /

Investiga las estaciones/Investigate the Seasons

Veamos la primavera/ Let's Look at Spring

por/by Sarah L. Schuette

Traducción/Translation: Dr. Martín Luis Guzmán Ferrer
Editor Consultor/Consulting Editor: Dra. Gail Saunders-Smith

Capstone press®

Mankato, Minnesota

Pebble Plus is published by Capstone Press,
151 Good Counsel Drive, P.O. Box 669, Mankato, Minnesota 56002.
www.capstonepub.com

Library of Congress Cataloging-in-Publication Data
Schuette, Sarah L., 1976–
    [Let's look at spring. Spanish & English]
    Veamos la primavera / por Sarah L. Schuette = Let's look at spring / by Sarah L. Schuette.
    p. cm. — (Pebble Plus. Investiga las estaciones = Investigate the seasons)
    ISBN-13: 978-1-4296-2289-9 (hardcover)
    ISBN-10: 1-4296-2289-X (hardcover)
    1. Animal behavior — Juvenile literature. 2. Spring — Juvenile literature. I. Title. II. Title: Let's look at
spring. III. Series.
QL753.S38218 2009
508.2 — dc22   2008004831

Summary: Simple text and photographs present what happens to the weather, animals, and plants in spring —
    in both English and Spanish.

Editorial Credits
Martha E. H. Rustad, editor; Katy Kudela, bilingual editor; Adalín Torres-Zayas, Spanish copy editor;
    Bobbi Wyss, set designer; Veronica Bianchini, book designer; Kara Birr, photo researcher;
    Scott Thoms, photo editor

Photo Credits
BigStockPhoto.com/George Muresan, 5
Corbis/Donna Disario, cover (background tree); Gabe Palmer, 20–21
Getty Images Inc./Stone/Andy Sacks, 10–11; The Image Bank/Harald Sund, 14–15
Peter Arnold/Hartmut Noeller, 6–7
Shutterstock/bora ucak, cover, 1 (magnifying glass); Clive Watkins, 1 (flowers); Danger Jacobs, cover
    (inset leaf); Radomir JIRSAK, 13; Shironina Lidiya Alexandrovna, 9
SuperStock/age fotostock, 19
UNICORN Stock Photos/Les Van, 17

The author dedicates this book to her friends Art and Barb Straub of Le Sueur, Minnesota.

Note to Parents and Teachers

The Investiga las estaciones/Investigate the Seasons set supports national science
standards related to weather and climate. This book describes and illustrates spring in
both English and Spanish. The images support early readers in understanding the text.
The repetition of words and phrases helps early readers learn new words. This book also
introduces early readers to subject-specific vocabulary words, which are defined in the
Glossary section. Early readers may need assistance to read some words and to use the
Table of Contents, Glossary, Internet Sites, and Index sections of the book.

Table of Contents

Tabla de contenidos

It's Spring!

How do you know
it's spring? Spring is
full of life.

¡Es primavera!

¿Cómo sabemos que
es primavera?
En la primavera todo
está lleno de vida.

Bright sunlight shines.
The next day rain falls.
Spring days are warmer
and wetter than winter days.

El Sol brilla con una luz
intensa. Pero, al día siguiente
puede llover. En primavera
los días son más cálidos y
más lluviosos que en invierno.

Sun and rain help plants
grow. Everything is
green again.

El Sol y la lluvia sirven
para que las plantas crezcan.
Todo se pone verde otra vez.

Animals in Spring

What happens to animals
in spring? Robins feed
their young in nests.

Los animales en primavera

¿Qué es lo que hacen
los animales en primavera?
Los petirrojos les dan de comer
a sus polluelos en los nidos.

Sheep graze in green pastures. Newborn lambs walk on wobbly legs.

Los borregos pastan en los pastizales. Los borreguitos recién nacidos caminan en sus tambaleantes patas.

Plants in Spring

What happens to plants in spring? Tulips bloom. Grass grows.

Las plantas en primavera

¿Qué les pasa a las plantas en primavera? Los tulipanes están en flor. La hierba crece.

Blossoms cover cherry trees.
Bees buzz in and out
of the flowers.

Los cerezos se cubren de
capullos. Las abejas zumban
dentro y fuera de las flores.

Planting begins on farms.
Rows of crops sprout
in fields.

En las granjas se inicia
la siembra. Los cultivos
brotan en los surcos
de los campos.

What's Next?

The weather gets warmer. Spring is over. What season comes next?

¿Qué le sigue?

El clima es cada vez más caluroso. Ha terminado la primavera. ¿Cuál es la siguiente estación?

Glossary

blossom — a flower on a fruit tree or other plant

crop — a plant grown in large amounts; corn, wheat, soybeans, and oats are some crops planted in spring.

graze — to eat grass that is growing in a field

pasture — a field of grass where animals graze

season — one of the four parts of the year; winter, spring, summer, and fall are seasons.

sprout — to start to grow

wobbly — unsteady

Glosario

brotar — empezar a crecer

el capullo — flor en un árbol frutal u otra planta

los cultivos — planta que crece en grandes cantidades; el maíz, el trigo, la soya y la avena son algunos de los cultivos que se siembran en primavera.

la estación — una de las cuatro épocas del año; el invierno, la primavera, el verano y el otoño son estaciones.

pastar — comer la hierba que crece en el campo

los pastizales — campo de hierba donde pastan los animales

tambaleante — inestable

Internet Sites

FactHound offers a safe, fun way to find Internet sites related to this book. All of the sites on FactHound have been researched by our staff.

Here's how:

1. Visit *www.facthound.com*

2. Choose your grade level.

3. Type in this book ID **142962289X** for age-appropriate sites. You may also browse subjects by clicking on letters, or by clicking on pictures and words.

4. Click on the **Fetch It** button.

FactHound will fetch the best sites for you!

Sitios de Internet

FactHound te brinda una manera divertida y segura de encontrar sitios de Internet relacionados con este libro. Hemos investigado todos los sitios de FactHound. Es posible que algunos sitios no estén en español.

Se hace así:

1. Visita *www.facthound.com*

2. Elige tu grado escolar.

3. Introduce este código especial **142962289X** para ver sitios apropiados a tu edad, o usa una palabra relacionada con este libro para hacer una búsqueda general.

4. Haz un clic en el botón **Fetch It**.

¡FactHound buscará los mejores sitios para ti!

Index

Índice